Home Movie

poems by

Charles Barasch

Finishing Line Press
Georgetown, Kentucky

Home Movie

Publisher: Leah Huete de Maines

Editor: Christen Kincaid

Cover Art: Photo by parent of Charles Barasch

Author Photo: Andrea Gould

Cover Design: Elizabeth Maines McCleavy

Order online: www.finishinglinepress.com
also available on amazon.com

Author inquiries and mail orders:
Finishing Line Press
P. O. Box 1626
Georgetown, Kentucky 40324
U. S. A.

Table of Contents

I
Rollerblading on L-DOPA

II
Bobby Richardson and Me

III

My Wife Puts on Her Bra

For Andrea

I

Rollerblading on L-DOPA

The Tidewater Motel

When the next Bible is written,
or the history of the world,
the Garden of Eden
will be the Tidewater Motel,
outside Ellsworth, Maine,
where the portable sign says
Blueberries and Lawn Ornaments,
Chocolates and Fishing Tackle,
Featuring Ruth and Wimpy's Kitchen,
Home of the $4.95 Lobster Supper,
where Wimpy with a busty Betty Boop
tattooed on his bicep, not a cheap one, either,
and, on his other arm, a woman with a snake,
stirs the lobster pot outside over a softwood fire,
and Ruth serves it all in the dining room,
with real wood paneling and pictures
of Elvis and John Wayne,
and paper placemats that tell you, wrongly,
the state bird of Maine is the bluejay,
and then gives you the key to #6,
where the concrete floor is covered
with a thin green carpet
and the glasses are sani-kleened
and the toilet seat has a ribbon around it,
and in the morning you can make love,
watch Sesame Street while you get dressed,
and give the key back to Ruth,
who'll bring you blueberry pancakes
while Wimpy gets the fire started,
while the sun rises over the ocean,
and the state bird, the chickadee,
whistles in the pines. Please make sure my
children know I have been there,
and my children's children.

At a Poetry Reading in a Congregational Church

I try to pay attention to the poet
but am distracted
by the image hanging
on the wall behind her:

Jesus, not hammered to a cross
as in a Catholic church,
but a portrait with glowing skin
and golden tresses, more beautiful
than handsome, his beard
like graffiti sketched
on a Veronica Lake movie poster,

a face to spark love and war,
inspire hucksters
and seducers, to carry
into battle emblazoned
on shields, and I wonder
if these good looks
come from his mother's
or his father's side.

New Hope Baptist Church, Newark, July

Four nurses in starched white,
hats moored to their heads like sailboats,
face the pews, fanning.
The choir, like picadors,
has roused the worshippers,
and the pastor takes the pulpit,
speaks in a voice so soft
no one is sure he has begun,
then jumps and lets loose a wail,
shakes a fist in the air,
and unfolds his fingers as if releasing
a dove. He claps and music soars
through the sanctuary, shifting
like a flock of birds through
upstretched, waving hands.
People dance, laugh, wipe sweat
from their brows and necks.
The nurses fan faster,
staying cool in case someone
begjns to ascend in the heat
or needs to be resurrected.

Jubilate Popcorn

Whoever saw the first kernel
sail into the sky from a hot rock
in the sun, perhaps,
must have thrown off his clothes and lain
wriggling in the grass, or done whatever
Holy Rollers did 5,000? 10,000?
years ago, and then run
into the village to tell everyone,
pointing to the heavens.
For nothing proves the existence
of God more than popcorn
(except, maybe, Christopher Smart's
electric cat Jeoffrey, and we know
Christopher Smart was crazy).

For there is no reason
popcorn should have evolved.
For it sizzles in hot oil and tries to reach God.
For it bangs against the pot.
For it gives off steam and sounds like thunder.
For it opens like a flower.

Getting Unstuck

for a young girl who stutters

When breath hides in your stomach
like a fish under stone
and, when it's hooked,
thrashes and teases,
dive down and follow.
Let it believe it's pulled you in
while you swim past swaying weeds,
through shadow and light.
When it thinks it owns you,
sing to it like a mermaid,
it will fall in love with you
and be your liveliest companion.
The home you set up together
will be happy until the end of your days.

Healing

"We want to heal you,"
the teenaged boy said as I gazed
from the 17th century monastery's
observation deck across
Cinque Terre to the Mediterranean.

From what? I thought, then realized
he'd seen me walking with my cane.
Five people encircled me.
The boy's father introduced
his wife, a younger son, a daughter.
"We're from Colorado," the father said.
"We'd be honored if you'd let us
heal you. Do you suffer from MS?"

"No, it's Parkinson's," I said. "You're
welcome to give it a try. Go ahead,"
but their hands were already fluttering over
my flowered shirt like a flock of birds.
The father implored Jesus
to free me from affliction, then asked
if I were Christian. I said, "No, Jewish."
He shrugged and said, "That's okay,
you never know. Thank you."
The family hugged me.
When I entered the gift shop
the wife was buying a postcard of St. Francis
surrounded by sparrows.

Rollerblading on L-DOPA

Once it kicks in, my arms swing
in time to my hips' sway,
and with the wind at my back,
a smooth stretch of blacktop,
I pirouette in my mind
like Charlie Chaplin
in *Modern Times*, defying
the forces of physics and aging,
accelerate out of the cul-de-sac
with reckless crossovers
and, turning home
before meds wear off,
relax, lean forward,
hands on thighs, and like
Derby Queen Joan Weston
after a jam, remove
my helmet, shake out luxurious
bleached tresses.

Early Spring in Vermont

There is only one thing to do
when your car sinks
to its axles
in mud.
Get out.
Close the door.
Kneel down
and start eating.
You will swallow
fern seeds
and mushroom spores,
eggs of millipedes
and ladybugs.
Soon, spring
will crawl around
inside you.
Then,
get on your bicycle.

Vermont, Late May

This year the phoebes are nesting
on the porchlight over my door.
Grasses and twigs hang down
like Spanish moss.
My house is a riverboat.
I stand on the porch,
pretending it's the ship's bridge,
singing *Swanee* into the dusk
while two phoebes sit in the oak,
flicking their tails impatiently,
caterpillars hanging from their mouths.
Frogs sing in the swamp.
I go inside leaving the porchlight off
and the phoebes settle into their watch.
The ship glides darkly into summer.

Nature App

Riding my bicycle,
I pass some little
orange and yellow flowers,
pull over and take a picture
for my nature app to identify.
I imagine the photo
zooming with a *whoosh*
to some guy sitting in a room
leafing through wildflower books,
wearing shorts, a flowered shirt,
a baseball cap. He knits his brow
as if planning a chess move
and, to keep his strength up,
slurps a milk shake
through a straw. I wonder
if he knows Siri—perhaps
they wave to each other
when they take out the garbage
on Monday mornings,
or maybe they met on a dating app.
A chime from my phone
announces his reply:
butter-and-eggs.

Labor Day

There is no wind today,
only the rasp of crickets hidden
in the grass, still green
after a wet summer.
Tiny legs churn like locomotives,
like the sewing machines
in a World War II newsreel,
so much clatter from the women
on the home front.
Each revolution of a leg
stirs a stalk—the same energy
stored in blackberries that bears
burn all winter, the energy
of armies marching across fields,
the energy we create with love.
There is so much heat
rising from the grass today.

On Our Dirt Road

A hay-crammed pickup truck,
bales stuck out each side,
bounces toward me
and my dog. The driver lifts
four fingers as he passes,
thumb still hooked around
the steering wheel, which is more
than the two fingers I raise,
or the index finger some people
offer, which beats out
the arched eyebrow.

One man extends his arm
each time someone drives by
while he's outside working,
rotates his hand backwards
about forty-five degrees,
and, continuing his business,
turns his back to you
because no one wants to seem too friendly
or unfriendly on our dirt road.

LaGuardia Airport

English sparrows trapped in the terminal
flutter from rafters
as *E lucevan le stelle,*
Mario Cavaradossi's
farewell aria from Tosca,
lovely and sad
like a veery's song
spiraling downward at dusk,
surrounds passengers awaiting
the flight to Washington.

The tenor switches to Wagner,
enters the men's room,
pauses to chatter with another janitor
and, to Mozart's *Dalla sua pace,*
swabs the floor by the urinals.
Then, singing Gilbert and Sullivan,
he's gone, a gondolier gliding
with his mop through the terminal
accompanied by a chorus
of swooping, chirping sparrows.

Mount Sinai Hospital E.R.

Hieronymus Bosch could have painted this:
a teenager and his parents argue with his girlfriend
who's already miscarried and stands doubled over
since there's no bed for her. Blood oozes
through her tight shorts, drips down her legs.
A man carries a baggie with a severed finger
which he uses to flip the bird
at anyone who looks at him,
a mother screams "Stop your crying!"
at a boy with a paper clip stuck up his nose.
Two policewomen wheel in a man
strapped to a bed. Plastic I.V. bags hang
above him like udders. An orderly shouts
"Make way!" but no one moves.

We have all been checked in
by the front desk nurse
sporting bright red lipstick and
a pink camellia in her hair.
I am here because I can't pee
six hours after day surgery.

When a guy I didn't even know was a cop
jumps on someone who's pulled a wallet
out of another man's pocket,
I find a men's room and finally
let go.

Le Dejeuner sur L'Herbe

It is a time she keeps calling back—
how she was bored
by the bread and the rotten cherries,
Manet exclaiming about exquisite,
eternal moments, photography,
posing her among the clothes and fruit,
her blue dress, her favorite petticoat,
and the sweat channeling down her thighs
making her want to run,
to cartwheel,
to give herself to the coachman
sleeping under the sycamores.

Les Nympheas

When I step back brushstrokes
find each other, dance,
meld into flowers and leaves.
Roots and stems sway underwater
like a choir, waves churn
and beat against me,
recede, beat again,
ancient blues and greens beckon,
suck me back to mud.
Slick, I curl and uncoil,
snake through lilies,
aware of each echoing breath,
tumble down, spiral to the surface.
On shore Monet chats with God
about how atoms became dust
and water, and dust and water
became stone and grasses and snakes.

Capriccio with St. Paul's and Old London Bridge, at the Met

The painting's perspective is so deep
and there is so much room under
the rounded Roman arch that I leap in,
and even though the museum's placard says
"the foreground is imaginary" bruise my knee
on the marble floor, my right knee,
the one that always gives me fits, anyway,
so when I lean forward into a straight-legged bow
and doff my feathered tri-corner to a passing lady
I lose my balance, brace awkwardly against a column
topped with a Corinthian capital,
and fall over the lower balustrade,
splash into the Thames, spray water across
the gallery. I swim toward St. Paul's Cathedral.
Someone points at me and grabs a security guard,
who says, "Don't worry, this happens all the time"
and pulls a life preserver from behind the painting,
throws it to me, hauls me out, hands me a towel.
I ask him where the Impressionists are,
and if the Seine is chilly
at Giverny this time of year.

Elegy for Mice

There have been many.
I carry the bodies outside
and, leaning over the fence,
unspring them,
depending on the season,
into a bed of snow,
or wild daisies,
lupines or asters.

Yesterday's lay on its side,
limbs stretched forward
like a bas-relief runner
on a Grecian urn.
Today's rested on its back,
well-fed and plump,
legs splayed open
like a confident pup
expecting a belly rub.

Its round black eyes
stared at me
after the night's carnage
with wonder, not anger,
like someone
who's received
nothing more
than a little bad news.

Goldfish Have a Memory of Three Seconds

(from a list of "little known facts" on a restaurant placemat)

Emma, my pet goldfish,
leads a fanciful life.
She keeps forgetting
what fog is, so in her world
it's easy to believe it comes
on little cat feet, or that
a man and a woman and a blackbird
are one, or that a pair of scissors
is two dancers twirling round,
lips finding each other
for staccato kisses,
or that a pineapple is a rocket ship,
or a head with green hair,
or a thatched hut with lattice windows
you can open to spy on
the little family inside.
Mother might be upstairs,
brushing her hair before the mirror.
Two children play go-fish,
the cat licks himself, and father
opens a beer in the kitchen,
where the goldfish in the bowl
on the counter has forgotten
how many of her children
she's eaten, much less their names.

Chatting with AT&T

"Do I get unlimited minutes
with the Mobile Share plan?"
"Yes," Bambi LaCroix writes back,
"and unlimited texting,
too. Can I sign you up?"
I ask, "Is Bambi your real name?"
and she responds, "Yes,
it's odd, isn't it? LOL"
and I want to say yes,
unless you have a white tail,
but type "OK, I'll take the plan."
She answers, "My mom liked the movie."
I write, "It scared me,"
and she answers "That's natural, fires
can frighten anyone. And of course,
no one likes to lose a mother.
Does that make sense?"
I write, "Yes, thanks,"
and she says "Is there anything else
I can help you with?"

40th High School Reunion

I'm afraid I'll get there and start bawling
when I see the Lindas, Susans, Davids—
no Natashas, Crystals, Dakotas in this crowd—
and they'll think it's because
I've missed them. I won't be able to say
No, it's because I don't think of you at all,
because forty years have gone by
faster than high school,
because the girl who played Wendy
in our *Peter Pan* production has grown up,
because it's at a hotel,
not the school gym with crepe paper
and balloons and shadowy
chaperones watching us slow dance,
because there'll be an open bar
and hors d'oeuvres, because
the invitation requested "business casual"
and I knew what that meant.

Ooh La La

Hungry, we checked the hotel room
mini-bar, found a $7 bag of gummy bears
and a red box decorated with hearts.
"Chocolates?" asked my wife.

"It's a Lovers Tryst Intimacy Kit," I said.
"You get two premium condoms,
Intimate Pleasures personal lubricant,
Breathless Mints, and an Ooh La La
Feather Tickler."

          "What do you imagine
you do with an Ooh La La feather tickler?"
she asked, laughing.

          "Tickle," I said.
"But I'd rather have a pillow fight."

"What I'd really like
are the gummy bears," she said.

We finished them off
and went back for the $8 m&ms.

"I'm satisfied," she said.

"Me, too," I answered.

A Session with Mary

My therapist, Mary, says to write
down my fears and worries,
and keep them in a folder.
That way, they'll always be available
when I need them.

        You never know
when you'll want to get one out
and cozy up to it, she says.
Then she asks which worry
I'd like to "explore" now.

I say I'm afraid of flying.

Too common, she says. Try something else.

OK, I'll go with a tick latching onto me,
sucking like a baby.

        A tick is nothing
like a baby, she yells.

        Are you angry at me?
I say quietly.

        Now we're getting somewhere,
she answers.

        We are?

        Oh, yes.
What are you really worried about?

I'm afraid my wife will leave me.

Everyone is. That doesn't count.

Let me try this. Sometimes
when I'm walking in a field
I imagine a tyrannosaurus appearing
out of the woods, hips rolling,
tiny arms flashing in the sun
like a wild chef sharpening
knives.

Wow! So do I.

And you're not going to believe this,
but when I think of chipmunks
I see grotesque faces
like close-ups of locusts
munching blades of grass,
each mouth wide open,
roaring like a crazy t-rex.

Exactly! she says. Don't get me started!

Impressing My Therapist

"Did I ever tell you I deejayed
an oldies show on the radio?" I say
to Mary, my fourth therapist of the year.

"Amazing," she says. "I never knew that."

The next session I tell her about
the bareback barrel race I won
riding a pinto mare.
"I got a blue ribbon big as Lord
Fauntleroy's tie. I still have it."

In the following weeks
I begin to make things up.
"I caught a home run
in the right-field grandstand
at Yankee Stadium, barehanded.
The crowd cheered as if
I were Mickey Mantle."

"I bet you didn't know I wrote
a computer program that finds
the rational roots of a polynomial
equation." I think this really wows her.

"I once won a pie eating contest."

"Charlie, you're incredible."

"Am I your favorite?" I ask.

"You're very special."

"But am I the most special?
Can't you just pretend?"

"Everyone brings their own unique story," she says.
"It's time to find a new therapist," I think.

Molasses Flood, 1919

Boston's great molasses flood sounds
like whimsy: sculls on the Charles
slog against the sweet tide,
men and women hopscotch
across Crackerjack cobblestones.

But bodies in workingman's tweed
are blown skyward, rivets explode
half a mile like bullets, a dark river,
fermented and rummy, surges
through streets, drags down horses,
pours into nostrils and lungs.

Maria Di Stasio and Patrick Breen,
clerks at Woolworth's on a lunch break stroll,
hear a roar, glance back and run
as the black wall rumbles
like a bull herd, chases
and covers them with treacle,
arms and legs flailing as if in quicksand
until she grabs his wrist
and slips her hand into his,
which is how they were found.

The Grump

Each autumn the handpainted sign
appeared in Abe Weinstein's
Tuscaloosa shoestore window:
"The Grump is Coming."
For the next week children
planned strategies to make him smile.
But the Grump had seen it all
(this was how he made his living)
and, on a crystalline afternoon
in 1938, thinking, perhaps,
of his wife in Birmingham,
he looked out from his folding chair
in Weinstein's display window.
Kids went crosseyed and stuck out
tongues, scratched like monkeys
or picked a buddy's nose.

A teenager showed up,
put his hands around his throat
and pretended to barf,
then began dancing. A throng
gathered round, whooping and clapping,
watching him jump and gyrate.
Even the Grump thought he was good
and, still stone-faced, made an "OK" sign
with his hand. The boy yelled, "Smile,
goddammit, smile," dropped his pants
and twitched his ass at the window,
but the Grump just frowned, until the boy
flung a rock through the pane,
shouting "Stupid Jew. Weinstein's
a stupid Jew!" and ran down the street
with a crowd that chanted "Jew! Jew! Jew!"
and hurled stones through Perlman's
shop window, then Levinson's.

II

Bobby Richardson and Me

Curveball

That curveball,
that terrible hummingbird,
dropped over the plate
so soft, *so real,*
like a pear or breast,
striking me out.

I love the pitcher.
I sit on the bench cursing him.

That curveball was the wheel,
was wine, was cooked food,
was Stonehenge.

World Series

Why, when Carlton Fisk
hit the home run,
did the man in Section 22,
down the third base line,
raise his hands for joy,
forgetting his sad wife
at home with the teenage daughter,
and driving home
why did he remember his wedding night,
and even the first night
parked by the river,
which is why he married her
in the first place?

I Was Glad My Grandma Was There

I was glad my Grandma was there
at Yankee Stadium
when the peanut vendor with no voice
came by. The other vendors shouted, *BEAH HEAH!*
and *SCORECARD YANKEE SCORECARD*
but he could only whisper, "Peanuts."

After the game, in the subway,
I held my Grandma's dress
while the train shook and screeched,
and looking out the window
into the dark tunnel
saw only my own reflection.
That night in bed I lay curled
with my knees to my chest.
I heard a crowd roar.
I felt myself becoming smaller and smaller
and was afraid I might disappear.

A Man and A Woman are Lying in Bed

His leg stretches
across her belly, his hand is a weight
on her breast.
In five minutes they might be making love,
or they might be asleep.

If ten years ago he hadn't turned down
a Rhodes Scholarship to play baseball
he might be living in a Tudor cottage
by a heath. This had been
one of his dreams.
If his arm hadn't broken down
in the minors
he might be in a hotel room,
trying to sleep, thinking of tomorrow's game.
If his boss's wife hadn't gone into labor
this morning, two months early,
he'd be at a meeting in Chicago.

If her husband hadn't left her
a year after they married—
if there hadn't been that party—
she'd be watching TV now
and there'd be two or three kids upstairs
sleeping. If her father hadn't gotten drunk,
hadn't been so insistent that night
with her mother in the Chevy,
and if her mother had taken *her* mom's advice
and gone to that doctor
in Puerto Rico . . .

Each of their lives has been a series
of miracles. Now their eyes meet.
Each thinks, "This is the moment
I've lived for."

When Ron Guidry Retired

For fifteen summers Mrs. Guidry planted the garden.
She pulled the weeds and kept away the deer.
She watched the sunset.
She talked with women.
She raised three children.

"I'm a little happy," she tells the reporters.
"A little sad—mostly sad.
I think Ron can still pitch."

In the newspaper photo she holds her newborn
and looks up at Ron saying farewell
at the microphone. In the staged lighting
she looks like the Virgin
in an old painting.
Her forehead glows, a shadow
runs along her nose and crosses her lips.
She is wearing a dark dress.

Secrets

Patty, when you became New York City's
1934 marbles champion, the first girl ever
to win, defeating the top boy
before 500 screaming children, knocking
nine out of thirteen ducks from the ring,
showing skill in long-distance plunking,
which the *New York Times* declared
"virtually impossible for a girl,"
did you decide right then
you'd keep this a secret?
And, later, when you played baseball,
barnstorming in buses through cornfields,
past factories, did you make plans
to bury away this part of your life?

Or was it the thirty years with Marguerite
in the suburbs that made keeping secrets natural,
the years you coached softball and smashed tennis balls
past college students too young to know
about adults loving each other,
so that when I rented a room
in your house one summer
I would never even wonder
whether you and Marguerite shared a bed?
Only after she died, and you showed me the photos,
you in bloomers carrying a baseball bat,
you and Marguerite camping in the '50s,
or walking a dog, did you teach your greatest lesson—
not just about the heyday of marbles
or the baseball glove in the attic trunk,
but how much you missed Marguerite,
how much you'd loved her.

Obituary

By the time Rick Anderson's heart gave out
he weighed over four hundred pounds.
He'd been the best pitcher on his high school team
and a minor league star, but in the majors
he threw only twelve innings, and walked
twice as many as he struck out.
After his arm went lame he lived
in a boatyard below Highway One
in a truck trailer with indoor plumbing
and no windows and a picture of himself receiving
the 1971 California high school
championship trophy. Day and night
he heard the ocean and seagulls
and downshifting gears, and sometimes
gravel spray in the boatyard or voices
of tourists. His parents came each Christmas.
When his body was found he was clutching a letter
containing five dollars and a request for an autographed
baseball card. He was thirty-five years old.

Bobby Richardson and Me

Imagine me, a ten-year-old
at Yankee Stadium
when Bobby Richardson hit a home run
just over the left field fence's 301 foot sign
as if he'd run out and deposited it by hand,
and not just any home run,
but a grand slam, and not just any game,
but the World Series, and not just any fan,
but a card-carrying—

> *it was in the pocket of the Yankees*
> *jacket I wore, that had been*
> *given to me by my grandmother,*
> *who was sitting next to me smoking*
> *Chesterfields, who had bought the tickets*
> *for god knows how much,*
> *and who, two years later*
> *at the same ballpark gave me*
> *my first sip of beer—*

member of the Bobby Richardson fan club
because, like me, he played
second base, and we were both serious
baseball players. We felt that turning
double plays was as important as hitting
home runs. We weren't flashy,
so what would he do with the Corvette
he won as the 1960
World Series Most Valuable Player?

I loved Bobby the same way
a few years later I loved
girls who didn't know I existed,
whose boyfriends dropped
used condoms out car windows
in the high school parking lot
while I listened to ball games

on the transistor radio
beneath my pillow.

Jim Spencer's Home Run

I was surrounded by other fans
at Fenway Park,
but from the moment
the ball left the bat
it seemed to pick me out,
fix on me like a guided missile.
I followed its arc
through the artificial twilight
and was surprised by
how softly it landed,
like a homing pigeon,
as if the two bare hands
it settled into were a nest.

Maestro

It seemed just another minor league stunt,
like between-inning sack races
and bat tosses, or the team's
mascot, a guy in a cow suit,
stomping on the opponents' dugout
with oversized hooves, then
leaning over to squirt the players
with water from his udders,
so when the paunchy coach jogged out
to sing the national anthem,
and people rose just as they had
for the off-key barbershop quartet
the night before, no one expected
his lovely tenor, each syllable pure,
unadorned, even the highest notes
reverberating strong and sweet.
Later, from his coaching box,
he sent runner after runner
careening around third,
his windmilling arm conducting them
home, his music echoing
through the ballpark.

The Ride

After the last *STEE-RIKE*, the players'
clickety-clack descent
through dugouts, into locker rooms
steamy with towel smacks and hip-hop,
fans in Yankees caps and shirts
shuffle around the Stadium, past hawkers,
through turnstiles under the street
and, as if sucked by a vacuum,
fill the D train. A man and woman
in Jeter jerseys speak Spanish,
stand, re-balance as the ride begins.
She leans against him, his arms
around her belly. Two Asian children
with baseball gloves giggle and pinch,
their parents gripping the rail overhead,
until the Latino man takes
the Asian woman's hand, kisses it,
and a woman whose husband holds
their toddler in full uniform on his lap
smiles at the Asian man and kisses *him,*
everyone falling in love,
as the train hurtles through its tunnel
bringing its riders closer
to where they've wanted to go.

III

My Wife Puts on Her Bra

My Wife Puts on Her Bra

You might think
this is too much sharing,
and my wife, who for this poem
I'll call Irene (which,
coincidentally,
is her real name),
would probably agree.
She opens a magical
drawer, takes out a bra,
and rather than pulling it
around herself the way someone
might put on armor, bends
forward, her back curved
like a swan's neck.
She lets her breasts
drop into it. I imagine
waterfalls, tympani.

Sewing a Nightgown for My Wife

It took twice as long to make
as it should have.
I admit that while I sewed
I was distracted by visions
of her taking it off,
so I could barely
keep my mind on the project,
twice misthreading
the sewing machine, misplacing
scissors, spilling
straight-pins all over.

Imagine if I'd attempted
a see-through nightie:
no doubt I'd have had her
try it on for size several times.
I might have punctured cloth,
ripped fabric and, probably,
attached the neck opening
to the bottom hem.

October Fog

for my wife Andrea on her 64th birthday

I dream I run with you
through recently thinned woods,
leading you around stumps
into mist-filled spaces between
trees, and point to a red leaf
stuck to a twig.
"It's like a perched bird," I say.
You flutter off, circle around maples,
sunbeams slashing like swords
through the haze.
"This is just like a dream," I say.
"But it's real," you say
and dive into the fog.
You emerge from a lake,
shaking off drops of water,
your hair brown, not silver,
parted in the middle
like it was in high school,
framing your face.
We hold hands across a table
in the school cafeteria.
Around us kids eat fries.
It's your birthday,
we are both seventeen.
Too shy to kiss you,
I wish we were 64
so I could say "I love you"
and you would know I've meant it
for all these years.

January 1

From bed you say the snow sifting down
is a show just for us. You say
I should write a poem about it. And about
the glittering ball we watched fall on TV
at midnight, and all the people kissing like crazy,
and how you didn't think the *New Yorker* cartoon
I showed you when you woke up was funny.
And I should put in a little darkness—
you know, the way Robert Frost did—
and I say why don't you write it yourself,
and you say, oh, no, but throw in something
about us turning 60 this year.
You say I can write the poem
when you go to yoga in an hour
and I can read it to you this afternoon
when we meet back in bed,
shades open, snow swirling in the wind.

Marine Disasters of Cape Cod

The poster, listing hundreds
of shipwrecks: *Nonpareil*, 1844,
Amethyst, 1847,
Anna Elizabeth, 1890,
St. Bernard, 1902,
hangs above the bed
in our rental cottage,
where one morning we argue
about the usual stuff,
continue as we walk on the beach,
sometimes brushing shoulders
by accident, until I take your limp hand,
which after a while folds around mine,
and when you point out a seal in the ocean
I turn to look, then kiss you,
a small one on your forehead.
The next morning we agree
on our favorite shipwrecks:
Olive Branch, 1801,
Harmony, 1859.
Neither of us cares for
Defiance, 1923,
or *I'm Alone*, 1957.

January Thaw

The woman who will give birth
to our child in the spring
watches from the kitchen window
while I kneel on sunflower husks
coming up like a plowed field
beneath the birdfeeder. A bear pauses
in the road, backs up to rub
against a budded maple.
Last night thunder and snow,
then rain. The south wind carries
the smell of last year's garden,
and by the stonewall the pine bends
and shakes like an emperor whose wife
has gone away, sailed
down the river, round the bend.

Perfection

for Anna

Let me describe a painting.
Green hills of wheat stretching
to the horizon. A deep blue sky.
A fiery sunset. Five puffy clouds
filled with letters of the alphabet
in perfect cursive the artist, my daughter,
is learning in school. O's, P's, C's, R's—
each loop precise, each curve perfect
as the arc of her arms around her head
in dance class. She cannot imagine making
anything more perfect than a lower-case "c."
She cannot imagine having to please
a lover curled around her back. She cannot
remember crying when her mother left home,
she only knows she must make things
perfect, she cannot imagine
a life without balloons, without
her pictures on the walls.

Blueberries

The blueberries are dying.
Young plants, four weeks in the ground.
The leaves are falling off.
The nursery can't tell me why.

My friends say I did everything right.
Broke up the soil, gave them a bed
of pine needles, knelt under the moon
to pray, to water them with tears,
and watch them grow.
I was afraid they were not happy enough.

It's like the time I married
a young girl. Washed her clothes.
Built a house around her. Fed her
until she disappeared.

Perennials

She had been gone three years.
The place had changed.
The path to the clearing was overgrown
with blackberries tangled like barbed wire.
He hadn't been there since they buried
the dog—he imagined
it was taken over by cedar and spruce
and even young maples.
And the view across the hayfield was gone.
The alders and chokecherries had sprung up
while he'd dreamt about her.

He put in poppies, phlox, lupine,
yarrow, primrose, mallow.
They needed light. He cut down trees
and cleared the brush. The sun crossed the sky
and set behind the mountains. The moon rose
and fireflies turned their lights on and off.
The perennials set out roots underground.
Each year they grew stronger, and multiplied.

Visiting My Father at the Nursing Home

A woman holding a full vase of flowers—
roses, tulips, lilies—
runs after me, scuffing
gravel. "Stop, sir, stop!" she shouts.

"The florist delivered these to
my house, but I don't want them.
Can you bring them to someone?"
Weeping, she hands over the flowers

as if she is giving away a baby,
walks back to her car and drives off.
I wave to her, but she looks straight ahead,
heads down the hill to town.

The young man with a heart balloon
tied to his wheelchair sits,
as usual, inside the nursing home
door like a guard.

"Would you like these
flowers?" I say, but he turns away.
I walk down the hall, past the woman
in a wheelchair whose chin

droops to her chest.
She doesn't want the flowers,
nor does the man wearing
headphones—I never can tell

if he is listening to something
or keeping noise out. My father
is asleep in his bed, but a woman
in the television room smiles at me

and takes the flowers. She brings them
to her face, takes a deep breath

as if recalling a lover, then removes
each petal, one by one.

The Little Boy

When my father was a little boy
his grandmother ran the household.
The key to the pantry
jangled from her apron.
There would be no snacks.
His mother lay in bed,
at times reading about Joan Crawford
or Greta Garbo in a movie magazine,
at times recovering
from electro-shock treatment.

The day before my father died
he threw his head from side to side
like a horse refusing a bridle,
avoiding the macaroni and cheese
I brought to his lips on a spoon,
so I said "Let's try the applesauce,"
but he clenched his mouth shut,
opening it just to say,
"I want my mother."

On the Morning My Father Died

After his body had been zipped
into a plastic bag and wheeled
from the nursing home,
the earworm that burrowed
through my brain as I got into
the car was *Davy Crockett.*
I began singing
*Born on a mountaintop
in Tennessee . . .*, and my wife
joined in, the two of us
going down the road,
. . . kilt him a bar . . .
and I interrupted and said,
"You know, one time
it was getting dark
and my dad called me in
for supper. I was playing
Cowboys and Indians with my friends.
He took my toy Winchester,
put on my hat, and joined the game.
I was embarrassed
but would give anything
to see him now
in that coonskin cap."

For the Children

The pork roast was never done.
Was this a ritual, turning down
the oven when we weren't looking
the way parents trick the kids
into believing in Santa Claus?
I never caught the wink when Dad said,
"It'll have to go back in," or when Mom
pretended to be annoyed.

Only now I realize you did it all for the children:
orange life jackets bobbing in Lake George,
roller derbies in the living room,
delivering Stevenson flyers in the red wagon,
the donkey and the bicycle built for two,
a stickball strike zone chalked on the house.

And the food we hated—liver, eggplant—
banishments to our rooms for teasing, even
your arguments were as much a part of your plan
as the night we brushed our teeth
before Terrytoon Circus and, after
Claude Kirschner told us *It's time
for all good boys and girls to go to bed,*
watched Gunga Din in our pajamas.
When Cary Grant peered into
the snakepit our family's shrieks
filled the house like a love song.

The Two of Them

When she could no longer
make herself understood,
my mother began talking louder,
bleating like an unsteady lamb,
my father circling around her,
protecting her from the howls of
relatives and friends who thought
things should change—move her bed
downstairs, perhaps, or hire a nurse.
They spent their days eating soup together,
irrigating catheters and counting pills,
arguing (in their own way,
since she could barely speak
and he was almost deaf),
the two of them alone and in love.

The Dance

After my father lifts and pivots her
into her chair, and wheels her to
the kitchen table, soup dribbles down
my mother's chin to her bib, trickles onto
her clean, pressed dress. She says something
that no one understands, puts down her spoon
and takes up a pen, my father hovering over
her once-proud cursive, pronouncing
each shaky word as it's written.

A young woman observes from the counter.
Black hair frames her lovely face, brushes
her embroidered cashmere sweater, lips open
and smiling: a photo of my mother at twenty.

From around the house she watches
at various ages: in a gown throwing rice
at a wedding, in flowered pedal pushers
playing softball, dancing at home
with my father, his hand on her back
guiding her through the kitchen.

Dream About My Family

The statue of Atlas on 5th Avenue
leans down, places the world
on my back, skips away laughing,
clicking his heels. I am ten years old,
it's mid-summer and I'd like
some Schrafft's ice cream
but can't get through the revolving door
with the world on my back,
and can't get into FAO Schwartz
to watch Lionel trains race through
tunnels and over trestles,
stopping to eject milk cans
the size of thimbles,
and can't go to the automat,
put a nickel in the slot,
open the door and, like a magician,
pull out a dish of creamed spinach.
Thousands of people stream
from coffee shops, dry cleaners,
druggists, and hop on the globe.
My shoulders droop
and my clothes drip with sweat.
I shout for everyone
to get off, and they do,
except my family,
who tighten their hold
and won't climb down.

Home Movie

A young woman sits in the background.
A man holds their baby,
presents him to the lens,
dances.
The camera follows,
the frame cuts past the woman.
We catch the side of her body,
legs bent under her,
the back of her head.
Her hand picks at the grass.
She is nineteen years old.

The woman rises, spreads her open palm
across the lens.
Her fingers appear on the screen,
a blur,
the camera shuts down.
There is an argument.
"He will love women too much," the man says,
"the way I love you."
The baby is crying in the grass.

Late December, in a Month the Temperature Never Went Above Freezing

How strange after coming home
through the dark forest
and stirring tea and honey,
to find I love myself as much as my father
loved me when I was two.
I sit quietly in the living room,
the pine walls creaking,
breathing, the shaggy fern
reaching to the window,
and the woman in the painting
stretched on her couch,
leaning on her elbow, reading,
her back curved against a pillow,
her round hip in sunlight,
her bowl of pears
always ripe and full.

ACKNOWLEDGMENTS

Many thanks to the journals, magazines and anthologies in which the following poems originally appeared, some in slightly different form:

Atlanta Review, "The Tidewater Motel"
Baseball, I Gave You All the Best Years of My Life, "Curveball," "I Was
      Glad My Grandma Was There," "Obituary," "When Ron Guidry
      Retired," and "World Series."
Cider Press Review, "My Wife Puts on Her Bra"
Epoch, "Curveball"
Harvard, "Vermont, Late May"
Hawaii Review, "Le Dejeuner sur L'Herbe" and "World Series"
Literary North, "Les Nympheas"
One Meadway, "Blueberries" and "January Thaw"
Proud Hands, "Rollerblading on L-DOPA"
Spitball, "Maestro" and "The Old Ballgame"
Tar River Poetry, "Chatting with AT&T" and "40th High School Reunion"

     I have been in a poetry group for over 30 years. Writers have come and gone, and there have been too many members to thank each of you individually. However, I thank you all for your critiques, comments, and editing of my work; I would particularly like to thank the current members: Nadell Fishman, Carol Henrikson, Sarah Hooker, Nicola Morris, and Diane Swan.

     Also by Charles Barasch: *Dreams of the Presidents*

Charles Barasch was born in Alabama. His parents brought him to New York when he was two years old and, eventually, to Vermont, where he has lived for 50 years. For over 40 of those years he was Moderator of the Plainfield town meeting. He worked as a speech language pathologist with young children and is now retired. He lives with his wife, Andrea, on a dirt road with a view of the mountains.

Barasch's poems have appeared in many journals, magazines, and anthologies, including *Atlanta Review, Harvard, Poet Lore, Tar River Poetry,* and the anthology *Baseball, I Gave You All the Best Years of My Life.* His book of poetry, *Dreams of the Presidents,* consisting of a dream-poem for each president, was published by North Atlantic Books. He has also written crossword puzzles for the *New York Times, Los Angeles Times,* and *Washington Post.*

CPSIA information can be obtained
at www.ICGtesting.com
Printed in the USA
BVHW040835270522
638300BV00006B/162

9 781646 628377